Developing Patience and Perseverance in an Impatient World

By SUSAN LEE

Copyright © 2018, 2016, 2013 by Susan Lee
All rights reserved. This book or any portion thereof may not be reproduced or used in any manner whatsoever without the express written permission of the publisher except for the use of brief quotations in a book review.

The information in this book is based on personal experience and opinion and is intended for general reference and should not be substituted for personal verification by users. The author and publisher disclaim any personal liability for the advice presented on these pages. All effort has been made to verify the accuracy of the information, but we assume no responsibility for errors, inaccuracies or omissions.

The Produce My Book Promise:

Our goal at ProduceMyBook.com is to provide you with a proven sequence of steps and sub-steps to learn and apply new skills...faster.

Authors benefit from our process by having a completed book to call their own, in as little as 8 weeks, without ever typing a word of the manuscript.

c/o Produce My Book
PO Box 441024
Aurora, CO 80044
ProduceMyBook.com/
crew@ProduceMyBook.com

CONTENTS

FREE BONUS

1	Introduction	1
2	Demonstrating Patience With Other People	7
3	The Ultimate Example of Patience	11
4	Strategies For Developing More Patience	19
5	Dealing With Conflict	25
6	Patience With Circumstances	29
7	Active vs. Passive Patience	35
8	Staying Optimistic While Enduring Trials	41
9	Overcoming Other Challenges	45
10	Discerning God's Will	49
11	Patience With Yourself	53
12	Standing Firm	59

FREE BONUS!

Thanks for purchasing *Developing Patience and Perseverance in an Impatient World*!

As a special gift for taking the time, I would like to provide you with access to **God's Law of Attraction Worksheets** which will help you determine your goals, create positive affirmations, and combat negative beliefs.

Also, you will receive two special collections, formatted for printing as reminder cards to be carried with you throughout the day:

Treasury of God's Promises is a collection of Bible verses that will help you focus on God's positive message.

Quotable Quotes is a selection of affirming quotes that will help you to keep God's powerful word in your heart.

In addition, you will be registered to receive new bonuses and gifts as they are added. To get all three gifts, just visit **ProduceMyBook.com/gloabonusreg.**

CHAPTER 1: INTRODUCTION

There was once a young man with big dreams. The boy knew his dreams came from God, but his family didn't agree.
His parents humored him. *"Sure, honey, you can do anything you want to in life."*

His brothers were not as understanding as his parents. They were quite angry that, according to the young man, they would bow down and grovel to the boy in the dreams he described. It was bad enough that their little brother was the favorite in the family, arriving when Dad had already made it and was reconciling to the fact that he probably wouldn't have any more kids. *"The child of my old age,"* Dad used to say.

He had turned 17, was almost a man. But Dad let him dress up in fancy clothes and kept him back from doing the hard work in the fields. What a sissy. Then one day, they found their chance to get even.

So begins the saga of Joseph, spanning many chapters of Genesis (Genesis 37, 39, 40, 41). Joseph's tale is one of the most revealing stories of how to demonstrate patience that the Bible tells. Amidst the drama of family jealousy, abuse, sex scandals, royal intrigue and natural disasters, Joseph's unwavering patience as he waited on God's will is a lesson for us all.

A lesson we seem to need every day of our lives.

I often wonder if the Bible has so many lessons for how to develop and demonstrate patience because it is such an unnatural way to think in this world. It seems like as soon as we set a goal, various obstacles start to get in the way, keeping us from achieving this aim. We, in turn, become impatient with other people, the situation, and even with ourselves.

Satan knows just where to strike once we've set a goal. And he uses our impatience as a prime way to keep us from focusing on and trusting God.

What happens when we are impatient? The symptoms evidence themselves in different ways for everybody. You may get upset and angry, quickly lose control and have bursts of temper and blame. You may burn out quickly or become pessimistic. Perhaps you will discard relationships, jobs, or organizations when things don't work out as you expected, or withdraw from a situation when you don't see immediate results. You may just go through life with an underlying dissatisfaction, never happy or joyful. Ultimately, impatience will lead to depression and the feeling that you just can't cope anymore.

Joseph certainly had the right to experience all these impatient feelings, and yet his story over the course of fifteen years tells another tale. Joseph suffered ridicule and verbal abuse from his brothers. Those same brothers eventually beat him up, threw him into a deep hole in the ground, and sold him to passing merchants for a few bucks.

Joseph's life got even more complicated. He became a servant in a prosperous home in Egypt, and dutifully performed his assignments until his master gave him a prominent position managing his household. Before long, the lady of the house got the hots for him and did her best to seduce him. When Joseph said no, she stole his clothes and lied, accusing him of attempting to rape her.

Thrown into bondage again, Joseph endured the indignities of prison life and made friends the best he could with his fellow inmates. Through this, Joseph kept the dreams that God placed in his heart alive and his eye on the goal. He probably still didn't see how he would become a great leader, but Joseph knew God had those plans for him, and he was willing to wait it out.

One day, Joseph used his ability to interpret dreams to help out a couple of fellow inmates who had previously worked in Pharaoh's palace. If his analysis was correct, their dreams foretold that the baker would hang in three days, and the Butler would be cleared of blame and restored to his previous position. Here is the part of the story where Joseph shows humanity that we can relate to. He begs the Butler to share his story and get Joseph out of jail already!

Was Joseph FINALLY demonstrating some impatience of his own by trying to mold the situation to his liking? Or was he merely using the tools available to him to play an active role in God's plan for him? We struggle with the same question in our lives, and, like Joseph, we may never know the answer. Because once Joseph's prediction came to pass and the Butler was restored, he forgot to remember Joseph, who wasted away in jail for another two years.

As you can read in the 41st Chapter of Genesis, Joseph's story does have a good ending. The Butler eventually remembered Joseph, and Pharaoh freed him from prison after Joseph interpreted the Pharaoh's dreams. The Pharaoh placed him in charge of all of his land to manage a coming famine. Joseph saved Egypt from starvation, reconciled with his family and they all lived happily ever after in Egypt.

How did Joseph endure those fifteen years and still come out on top? Any one of the many trials he encountered over the years could have been enough to send him over the edge. But instead, Joseph remained patient with his life, the people around him, and with God.

What is patience? Just waiting for something to happen doesn't accurately define patience. If I have a good book, I can sit and wait for as long as is needed. That doesn't make me patient, however, because the wait isn't uncomfortable or troubling at all.

Dictionary.com defines patience *as the bearing of provocation, annoyance, misfortune, or pain; without complaint, loss of temper, or irritation*. But the story of Joseph, together with many other lessons in the Bible, teaches us that patience is not merely tolerating trials as a matter of necessity. Patience is enduring through a tenacious determination of will; to resolutely overcome the negative things we encounter, according to God's will.

Joseph didn't passively ignore his situation or quietly accept his lot in life. He remembered at all times that the Lord was with him (see Genesis 39:2-3, 21, 23) and that He had a plan for Joseph's life. With that in mind, Joseph was able to endure the times of trouble, stress, need, and anger, and remain faithful to stay the course.

The Bible uses these other phrases also to describe a patient spirit: *slow to anger, long-suffering, enduring and persevering*. The dynamic characteristics of each of these phrases suggest that merely waiting won't improve our fortune faster. We will still struggle with our children, look for more money at the end of our paycheck and have to wait for that annoying family in front of us at the supermarket.

But what these do hint at is an optimistic persistence caused by a peaceful mental attitude that helps us to be relaxed rather than frenzied while we wait. We don't 'check out' of life; we sincerely look for opportunities to pursue our goals. With optimistic persistence, a delay becomes more tolerable, and a job becomes easier. We are productive and enjoy the process more when we are patient with our circumstances.

In Luke 18:1-8, we read:

Jesus told them a story showing that it was necessary for them to pray consistently and never quit. He said, "There was once a judge in some city who never gave God a thought and cared nothing for people. A widow in that city kept after him: 'My rights are being violated. Protect me!'

He never gave her the time of day. But after this went on and on he said to himself, 'I care nothing of what God thinks, even less what people think. But because this widow won't quit badgering me, I'd better do something and see that she gets justice—otherwise I'm going to end up beaten black-and-blue by her pounding.'"

Then the Master said, "Do you hear what that judge, corrupt as he is, is saying? So what makes you think God won't step in and work justice for his chosen people, who continue to cry out for help? Won't he stick up for them? I assure you, he will. He will not drag his feet. But how much of that kind of persistent faith will the Son of Man find on the earth when he returns?"

The above story suggests three different types of patience that we should all work toward developing in our lives: patience with other people, with our circumstances, and finally, with ourselves. We will explore each of these further in the coming Chapters.

CHAPTER 2:
DEMONSTRATING PATIENCE WITH OTHER PEOPLE

Since God chose you to be the holy people he loves, you must clothe yourselves with tenderhearted mercy, kindness, humility, gentleness, and patience. Make allowance for each other's faults, and forgive anyone who offends you. Remember, the Lord forgave you, so you must forgive others. (Colossians 3: 12-13)

Demonstrating patience with other people can be one of the most powerful examples of God's love for us. As the Golden Rule teaches, we are to do to others as we would like others to do to us. I can't think of any instance where I wouldn't want other people to treat me with kindness, compassion, and especially patience. As God's children, our patience affects our ability to be a positive example and to share God's message with the world.

Knowing that, unfortunately, doesn't make being patient with other people any easier! The truth is, some folks will try your patience regularly. It's tough to get along with someone who continually interrupts what you are saying, bothers you at work, has terrible timing or tells boring story after boring story.

Sometimes, our impatience with other people injures no one but ourselves, such as the silent, petty impatience with perfect strangers we experience throughout the day. For example, how many times have you secretly fumed at a very slow customer you got stuck behind in the grocery store? Do you think he realized how annoyed he made you?

I am a very fast walker, so one area where I am challenged to keep my patience is when I get trapped behind a bunch of slower walkers. They may be having a great time meandering down the walk, catching up on a conversation, but I am immune to their good times. I bounce on my toes like an Olympic sprinter, waiting and watching for any opening where I can squeeze in and pass the inconsiderate horde.

The fact of the matter is that your anger and impatience toward those loud people at the next table or the teenagers that rammed into you on the bus don't affect them in the least. They are oblivious and, while rude; they aren't out to get you personally. Most of the time, we just endure it silently. But instead of letting it go, we can let these nuisances build until our whole attitude is damaged.

God teaches us to release the negative emotions that these petty annoyances can cause and to set our minds on more constructive endeavors:

And now, dear brothers and sisters, one final thing. Fix your thoughts on what is true, and honorable, and right, and pure, and lovely, and admirable. Think about things that are excellent and worthy of praise. (Philippians 4: 8)

Most often, our impatience is directed not to the strangers on the street, but toward our friends, family, and co-workers, which can negatively affect our relationships and lead to unresolved conflict.

God wants us to treat others with the respect and empathy they deserve as children of God. As annoying as people may be, they are important and unique to God, made in His image. Every one of us has immeasurable valuable, just because He created us.

Demonstrating patience with other people helps develop understanding, empathy and compassion. Part of being patient is to learn to work out our conflicts. Patient people take the time to process what they go through and identify which things that bother them are valid and need attention, and which are petty and picky. This results in better, more fulfilling relationships with spouses, friends, children and bosses.

People with understanding control their anger; a hot temper shows great foolishness. (Proverbs 14:29)

Impatience with another person often occurs when we think that person is in some way hampering our goals. We may even believe they are challenging or condemning us; we aren't feeling support for our desires, so we get annoyed and impatient.

The truth of the matter is that we all approach life from a different perspective, but for each and every person that perspective has 'me' in the center. All other individuals and circumstances ripple out from that center.

Our goal as Christians is to learn to take 'me' from the center of our perspective and replace it with 'God.' On the occasions we can pull that off, our first reaction to an irritating person is not to complain about them verbally or internally, but to deal with the situation with optimistic endurance. Doing so creates more patience and compassion; we learn to overlook their shortcomings, knowing that we probably have a few of our own!

The ability to replace 'me' with 'God' and to deal with annoying people with patience doesn't happen overnight. Like a bodybuilder must work out their muscles to grow stronger, we need to take the time to develop our patience toward other people. Chapters four and five will give you some tips and techniques to help you to build that strength.

CHAPTER 3:
THE ULTIMATE EXAMPLE OF PATIENCE WITH OTHER PEOPLE

And remember, our Lord's patience gives people time to be saved. (2 Peter 3:15)

The greatest example of patience that we could emulate is Jesus Christ. Surely Christ had a lot of circumstances in His life requiring patience, such as enduring the shame, ridicule and torture He did to die on the cross.

While Jesus' patience towards His disciples is less obvious, it's no less important as we learn to be patient with other people.

The truth is, although Jesus could have picked anyone to be His disciples, the men he chose were very 'human' indeed. Some of them were simple fishermen. Matthew was a tax collector who cheated and hung out with sinners. Simon the Zealot was what we would call a religious fanatic today. None of the men were great theologians or scholars. They often made mistakes and had doubts and lapses in faith all the time. In a nutshell, Jesus's disciples were ordinary people, just like you and me!

And yet, Jesus patiently trained these regular guys over the course of His ministry to become mature men of faith. It wasn't easy as these rookies were often confused as to who Jesus was and habitually misunderstood His mission. Here are a few great examples of the patience Jesus demonstrated.

James, John, and Mom

As Jesus was speaking about the things that were to come, Zebedee's wife, whose sons were among Jesus' disciples, came to Jesus with her sons and knelt down before Him to ask a favor.

Jesus: *What do you want?*

Zebedee's Wife: *When the kingdom of God is made manifest, I want one of my boys to sit at Your right hand, and one to sit at Your left hand.*

Jesus (to all three): *You don't understand what you are asking. Can you drink the cup I am going to drink? Can you be ritually washed in baptism just as I have been baptized?*

Zebedee Brothers: *Of course!*

Jesus: *Yes, you will drink from My cup, and yes, you will be baptized as I have been. But the thrones to My right and My left are not Mine to grant. My Father has already given those seats to those for whom they were created.*

The other ten disciples learned what the Zebedee brothers had asked of Jesus, and they were upset. So Jesus called the disciples together.

Jesus: *Do you want the Kingdom run like the Romans run their kingdom? Their rulers have great power over the people, but God the*

Father doesn't play by the Romans' rules. This is the Kingdom's logic: whoever wants to become great must first make himself a servant; whoever wants to be first must bind himself as a slave— just as the Son of Man did not come to be served, but to serve and to give His life as the ransom for many. (Matthew 20:20-28, The Voice)

Are you a high achiever? If you are, this story is for you, and can teach a real lesson in the difference between tolerant leadership versus plain old ambition.

Here we have the stuff of soap operas. Two of Jesus' disciples and their mother attempt a power play for preferential treatment in the Kingdom of God. James and John were cousins of Jesus, so that may be why they thought they had the right to make such a request. But the other disciples didn't see it that way and were not happy about it!

The problem, of course, was that the disciples still didn't understand that God's Kingdom was not a worldly place. Even after all the time and patience Jesus had taken to teach them about the Kingdom of God and His coming death, they still didn't get it. They were thinking of a worldly kingdom - gold thrones, servants and their place next to the indestructible king, Jesus.

Difficult to believe? Maybe.

My husband was a little league baseball coach for several years. He just loved finding the ball player's hidden talents and passions. The people that were hard for him to work with, however, were the parents. He would spend hours figuring out the right field positions and batting orders for the game, only to have to deal with an eager parent who wanted to see their boy play a particular position or more innings.

These pushy parents weren't bad people; they were just looking out for the player that was most important to them.

Unfortunately, they didn't see the big picture and didn't understand that their ambitions for their sons didn't fit into the overall plan for the game. A little bit like the disciples, hm?

Now I think it is safe to say that James and John were not evil, power hungry men. After all, they were hand-chosen to be Jesus' disciples. But they were human, and in being human, they made human mistakes: First in misunderstanding what God's kingdom was, and second by seeing themselves in the center of the more worldly kingdom they were picturing - full of power, riches, and influence.

Knowing that not only was Jesus fully God, but also fully human, I wonder what Jesus' human reaction to James, John, and even the other disciples' righteous objections would have been. We may never know, except to compare it to how we might react in the same situation. But instead of lashing out in impatience as we might, Jesus demonstrated perfect patience. Notice he didn't reproach James or John for their high-reaching request, or the other disciples for their less than loving response; instead, he turned the situation into another opportunity to teach the disciples about the real kingdom of God.

Thomas and Philip's Confusion

Thomas: *Lord, we don't know where You are going, so how can we know the path?*

Jesus: *I am the path, the truth, and the energy of life. No one comes to the Father except through Me. If you know Me, you know the Father. Rest assured now; you know Him and have seen Him.*

Philip: *Lord, all I am asking is that You show us the Father.*

Jesus (to Philip): *I have lived with you all this time, and you still don't know who I am? If you have seen Me, you have seen the Father. How can you keep asking to see the Father? Don't you believe Me when I say I abide in the Father, and the Father dwells in Me? I'm not making this up as I go along. The Father has given Me these truths that I have been speaking to you, and He empowers all My actions. Accept these truths: I am in the Father, and the Father is in Me. If you have trouble believing based on My words, believe because of the things I have done.* (John 14:5-11 The Voice)

For over two years, day by day, Jesus had been showing his apostles that he was the spitting image of God the Father. In fact, he was God the Father; His words and actions, his thoughts, his emotions, his purpose and his spirit all revealed that of His Father in Heaven.

And yet Philip says, "Lord, show us the Father, and that will be enough for us," like he hasn't been looking at him in the face for two years. Jesus answers Philip, "Anyone who has seen me has seen the Father. If you can't believe what I say, at least believe what I've done."

In other words, "It may seem bold of me to say so, but how else do you explain how I was able to cure the sick, feed five thousand, and even raise Lazarus from the dead?"

I have a small human glimpse of how Jesus must have felt. Exhibit number one: my husband who, despite the fact that I never wear his shoes or drive his car, seems to think I know exactly where all of his belongings are at any given moment. If something is missing, he calls out "where is my _____?" and then stands there waiting for me to find it.

Nine times out of ten the "missing" item is staring him right in the face if he'd just bother to take a look. He may not be asking me where God the Father is, but, as Thomas and Philip, he is blind to something that is right in front of his eyes. Judging by how quickly I lose my temper with him, it's unbelievable to me that Jesus could be so patient and understanding with their ignorance over a much more important matter.

In the Garden

It is indeed a dark, bitter night. The disciples are sad and confused, and maybe a little bit prideful. Peter cannot believe that he could ever betray his Lord.

At that, Jesus led His disciples to the place called Gethsemane.

Jesus: *I am going over there to pray. You sit here while I'm at prayer.*

Then He took Peter and the two sons of Zebedee with Him, and He grew sorrowful and deeply distressed.

Jesus: *My soul is overwhelmed with grief, to the point of death. Stay here and keep watch with Me.*

He walked a little farther and finally fell prostrate and prayed.

Jesus: *Father, this is the last thing I want. If there is any way, please take this bitter cup from Me. Not My will, but Yours be done.*

When He came back to the disciples, He saw that they were asleep. Peter awoke a little less confident and slightly chagrined.

Jesus (to Peter): *So you couldn't keep watch with Me for just one short hour? Now maybe you're learning: the spirit is willing, but the body is weak. Watch and pray and take care that you are not pulled down during a time of testing.*

With that, Jesus returned to His secluded spot to pray again.

Jesus: *Father, if there is no other way for this cup to pass without My drinking it—then not My will, but Yours be done.*

Again Jesus returned to His disciples and found them asleep. Their eyes were heavy-lidded. So Jesus left them again and returned to prayer, praying the same sentiments with the same words. Again He returned to His disciples.

Jesus: *Well, you are still sleeping; are you getting a good long rest? Now the time has come; the Son of Man is just about to be given over to the betrayers and the sinners. Get up; we have to be going. Look, here comes the one who's going to betray Me.* (Matthew 26:36-46 The Voice)

This story doesn't need much explanation of Jesus' extreme patience with his disciples, particularly for those of us who have trouble staying up late at night. I can't count the number of times I have fallen asleep watching a movie only to be awoken by flying objects like pillows and wadded up paper thrown by my annoyed husband and kids!

Jesus had asked His disciples to stay awake to support Him not only in prayer but by just being there during what would be His most challenging trial. That's a little bit more important than watching a movie.

But, did Jesus lose it and throw things or yell at the disciples? No, He understood with quiet patience. And, because Jesus was at peace, He was able to accept what His disciples did offer Him, limited as it was.

These stories remind us that we need to thank Jesus for His patience with us for our lack of knowledge and understanding of Him, just like He was patient with His disciples. But we should also use His examples to practice the fruit of patience in our lives.

CHAPTER 4:
STRATEGIES FOR DEVELOPING MORE PATIENCE WITH PEOPLE

Make every effort to live in peace with everyone and to be holy; without holiness, no one will see the Lord. (Hebrews 12:14)

Do all that you can to live in peace with everyone. (Romans 12:18)

We are encouraged to deal with people with patience and understanding because it puts our witness on display in a very tangible way. That can be hard! So it is a good idea to fill your toolbox with techniques for releasing the negative thoughts that you experience about other people. Doing so will open room in your heart and mind for God's comfort and support that is so desperately needed to demonstrate patience. Here are a few ideas to help release that negative energy and build your tolerance towards others.

Releasing

Here is a simple exercise you can use to help release the negative energy that happens when you get annoyed or impatient, providing room for more positive, empowering thoughts.

<u>Awareness</u>. First, become aware of your feelings. What sensations and emotions are going on inside you? Are you uncomfortable, doubtful, upset, peeved, frustrated, or angry? Try to give voice to the actual feelings you are encountering.

<u>Acceptance</u>. Let the unwanted feeling rise to the surface of your awareness. Feel it completely - don't push it back into your subconscious. Be aware of the feeling and accept it. Tell yourself, just as if you were counseling a friend, that it's okay to have that feeling.

<u>Let Go</u>. Finally, let go! Let go of the unwanted feelings and energy. Let them flow out of your body. Visualize the negative feelings leaving you by creating an image of that release. For example, you may want to picture a teakettle letting off steam, or a water dam breaking and the water gushing over the edge. I like to imagine a funny cartoon character exploding like in a Roadrunner cartoon. Use whatever will work for you to release completely the negative feelings you have.

Go through this exercise as many times as you need to fully release the negative emotions. You will probably find that each time you go through it, the negative feelings will lessen a little bit more.

If you practice the exercise whenever you feel tense and impatient, it will become easier to let go of the negative feelings quickly. Eventually, you won't even have to go through the steps consciously, and will instead jump right to your release visual.

Softening

Imagine you have a customer that just does not have it

together. He is slow getting you the details you need to finish a task for him and the information he sends you is incomplete. You end up spending a lot of your time looking for his errors and correcting his work. That takes you away from tasks for other customers that you had planned.

When you are talking to yourself and others, what words would you use to describe this client? If your descriptions are full of negatively charged words, you will create much stronger emotions than if you can soften the emotional impact of the words you choose. Proverbs 15:1 says *"A gentle answer deflects anger, but harsh words make tempers flare."* While this is most definitely right about what we say to others, we often forget that the words we speak to ourselves have a tremendous impact as well. Choosing kinder, gentler words throughout your day can help you develop the patience you need to deal with difficult people.

For example, read the following sentences and let yourself feel the emotions that arise when using the different words:

1. It infuriates me that I have to re-do his work every time.
2. I get annoyed when I have to re-do his work every time.

1. She is so rigid it makes me angry!
2. Her determination can be irritable at times.

1. That moron got these figures wrong again.
2. He sure can be distracted - he got these figures wrong again.

Do you notice how the first sentence stirs up negative emotions within you while the second softens them? People will be annoying - it is a fact of life. But by using less emotionally charged words to describe your negative reactions to people, you are looking at the world through God's eyes, not Satan's, which will develop peace of mind and harmony. That is a state that is much more helpful in building patience with people.

Another trick I suggest when using this technique is to find a "softened" word that you think is amusing. For example, when I feel myself becoming angry or upset, I use the word "peeved." It's such a silly word that I find myself smiling a little, and the negatively charged emotions that were stewing up inside me instantly calm. Try to come up with words like that to soften emotions that you often feel.

Here are a few possible suggestions for softened words:

I feel humiliated - - - I feel perturbed

I feel controlled - - - I feel hassled

I feel manipulated - - - I feel hoodwinked

I feel ignored - - - I feel tuned out

I feel punished - - - I feel scolded

You can come up with your set of replacement words that soften those negatively charged words that you find yourself using over and over again.

Become an Inverse Paranoid

One last technique is to practice what Jack Canfield likes to call "inverse paranoia." For developing patience with other people, inverse paranoia means that instead of thinking that that an annoying person is plotting to do you harm, you should instead believe that they are planning to do you good. Or, at the very least, be aware that everyone is dealing with struggles, weaknesses, setbacks, and obstacles. It is not all about you.

Practicing inverse paranoia shifts the focus from "what's in it for me" to a collaborative mentality that can benefit everyone involved. Imagine how much easier it would be if everyone went through life expecting other people to support them and build them up, rather than worried about how to save their skins. And the good news is that when you start practicing inverse paranoia, people around you will change and practice it as well. That is why Paul inspires the Thessalonians to *"encourage each other and build each other up, just as you are already doing."* (1 Thessalonians 5:11). What goes around, comes around!

CHAPTER 5:
DEALING WITH CONFLICT

No matter how patient and understanding you become, you will experience conflict with others from time to time. God's word teaches us that it is always best to deal with conflict through understanding and love:

A gentle answer deflects anger, but harsh words make tempers flare. (Proverbs 15:1)

But the wisdom from above is first of all pure. It is also peace loving, gentle at all times, and willing to yield to others. It is full of mercy and good deeds. It shows no favoritism and is always sincere. And those who are peacemakers will plant seeds of peace and reap a harvest of righteousness. (James 3:17-18)

Experts agree there are five methods for dealing with conflict as it arises:

1. Attack! Attacking is the least effective method and the most contrary to how God wants us to behave in this world. When we attack, we lash out aggressively at the conflict and the person.

Because emotions and adrenaline are high, it is very tempting to use this method when dealing with conflict. But keep in mind that the source of the conflict is Satan, who loves to stir up trouble. When negative, hurtful emotions are present in a situation, Satan slithers in and makes it even worse.

The good news is, Satan doesn't have any ammunition against gentleness, compassion, understanding or love. If we can learn to deal with conflict using these tools, his meddling will be obstructed, and God's love can get to work.

2. Avoid. When you avoid conflict, you are running away from it. Your hope is not to resolve it, but for it to just go away altogether. While this approach is preferable to attacking, it doesn't get to the root of the conflict. Often, you don't avoid it at all - you just move the conflict inside of you. You feel hurt and wronged, spend lots of time and negative emotion thinking about the conflict, and may even subconsciously look for ways to get even with the other person.

The final three methods for dealing with conflict are much more productive and preferable in God's eyes. Also, they will bring you more peace of mind. Each has its useful place, depending on your relationship with the person.

3. Walk Away. While this method may appear similar to "avoid," it is entirely different. When you walk away from a conflict, you are consciously deciding that it does not affect your goals, and it is not important enough to give attention. So you just let it go and forget about it.

When you develop the ability to walk away from a petty or inconsequential conflict, you develop a positive reputation for being even-minded and understanding. You are better able to manage your time and emotions and stay focused on your purpose in life.

4. Prevent. You may be able to anticipate the potential conflict and take action to prevent it before it even occurs. This strategy is different than "avoid" or "walk away" because you are proactive. It is a preemptive resolution! When you prevent a potential conflict, you are better able to develop high-quality solutions and demonstrate excellent leadership qualities. Here are a few ideas to prevent conflict:

<u>Don't allow a minor argument to turn into a big one</u>. To do this, you have to be able to step back, analyze your emotions and make the commitment to find a solution to what is bothering you and the other person.

<u>Analyze expectations in advance</u>. Conflicts often develop when someone has unmet expectations. If communication with someone is getting rough, take a step back and try to determine what the other person expected that didn't happen.

<u>Recognize that the other person is looking at the world with different perceptions than you are</u>. Everyone sees things a little differently based on their background, personality, and culture, and if this isn't understood, then you may not be able to prevent conflict.

<u>Recognize that mistakes happen</u>. Sometimes, people just make unintended errors. Before blowing up, do a reality check and ask yourself if what is bothering you could be the result of a mistake. If you made a mistake, apologize and work toward correcting it. If it is the error of the other party, identify it objectively and work toward correcting the mistake and preventing a conflict.

5. Resolve. Finally, if you can't walk away from or prevent the conflict, you must take action to investigate the source, use problem-solving skills, and try to find a solution that works. By taking the initiative to resolve conflicts when they arise, you reduce stress, create positive rather than negative energy, and improve your relationships. Here are a few ideas to assist in resolving conflict:

<u>Commit to working it out</u>. A positive impact will instantly result when you promise to find a resolution. It can turn a negative situation positive immediately.

<u>Ask Questions</u>. Most of the time, the conflict occurred because of poor communication. As part of your goal to resolve the dispute, ask lots of questions, which will help to get to the root of the conflict and resolve it much more quickly.

<u>Eliminate the E's</u>. Do not allow exaggerations, embellishments, or egos to get in the way of working toward a resolution.

CHAPTER 6:
PATIENCE WITH CIRCUMSTANCES

In every Christian's life, there comes a time when we must wait for some 'thing' to happen. Patience of this type asserts itself in two main ways: waiting to achieve a goal and enduring a trial. There is frequent overlap between the two, but the key thing is that in both circumstances, our impatience is not directed outward towards others, but upward towards God.

Just as we get annoyed when our children can't wait for us, I imagine this bothers God. A lot. But we can give thanks that His response to us is to give us another chance, and another, and another. *The Lord is slow to anger and filled with unfailing love, forgiving every kind of sin and rebellion. (Numbers 14:18)*

It is often said that the lessons we learn and the person we become while enduring a trial of circumstance can mold us into a better and stronger Christian. In fact, James tells us to consider these trials a joy: *When troubles come your way, consider it an opportunity for great joy. For you know that when your faith is tested, your endurance has a chance to grow. So let it grow, for when your endurance is fully developed, you will be perfect and complete, needing nothing. (James 1:2-4)* One thing is sure: we can all use some continuing education on building our patience with trying circumstances.

Waiting to Achieve a Goal

Perhaps you want to start a business, lose weight or find a mate. Or you may dream of earning a million dollars, starting a charity, or climbing a fourteener. There are as many possible goals as there are people on this earth, and God has given us all the desire to strive for the things we don't have: *Delight yourself in the Lord, and he will give you the desires of your heart. (Psalm 37:4)*; and *But as for you, be strong and courageous, for your work will be rewarded. (2 Chronicles 15:7).*

Despite your best efforts, it hasn't happened the way you had hoped yet, which is frustrating, especially when Satan is so quick to show you other people that are making it big time in whatever area you have set your goal.

What happened to "For I know the plans I have for you..." (Jeremiah 29:11) you wonder. Did God forget about me? Worse, does he just not care? Even worse, is he out to get me? Despite our commitment to walk with the Lord, most of us have whispered these same questions at one time or another when our dreams haven't happened at the speed and intensity we want them to.

"Timing is so important! If you are going to be successful in dance, you must be able to respond to rhythm and timing. It's the same in the Spirit. People who don't understand God's timing can become spiritually spastic, trying to make the right things happen at the wrong time. They don't get His rhythm – and everyone can tell they are out of step. They birth things prematurely, threatening the very lives of their God-given dreams." T. D. Jakes

We often forget that God's timing is not necessarily our

timing. Just because we think something should happen by a particular time, that doesn't mean our worldly goal fits in with God's heavenly plan. We know that God loves us and wants to give us the desires of our hearts, but it is often so hard not to grab onto the controls and try to make it happen on our own. We need a good deal of patience in these situations. It helps to remember at these times that God's Word is full of his promises of perfect timing:

Then the Lord said to me, "Write my answer plainly on tablets so that a runner can carry the correct message to others. This vision is for a future time. It describes the end, and it will be fulfilled. If it seems slow in coming, wait patiently, for it will surely take place. It will not be delayed. (Habakkuk 2:2-3)

The Lord isn't being slow about his promise, as some people think. No, he is being patient for your sake. He does not want anyone to be destroyed but wants everyone to repent. (2 Peter 3:9)

No, dear brothers and sisters, I have not achieved it, but I focus on this one thing: Forgetting the past and looking forward to what lies ahead, I press on to reach the end of the race and receive the heavenly prize for which God, through Christ Jesus, is calling us. (Philippians 3:13-14)

So let's not get tired of doing what is good. At just the right time we will reap a harvest of blessing if we don't give up. (Galatians 6:9)

Enduring a Trial

Sometimes bad stuff just happens to us that requires our patient endurance. Maybe you or someone you love is going through a dangerous illness, has been laid off or is suffering an addiction. Perhaps you are still looking for your soul mate or are unable to conceive a child.

Being patient through a trial can be very hard. Physical and mental limitations keep our negative vibrations in focus and push our natural positive emotions back. It's hard to see how God is working in the situation and, unlike working toward a goal, it often seems as though there is little we can do to improve it.

The sobering truth is that the world is full of sin, and because of that, life will be hard at times. To be patient at these times, we need to prepare ourselves in advance and accept that things won't always go as we wish or plan.

I was taking a hike with my daughter a few months back, and we came to a river crossing. We stopped for a while, and my daughter discovered some beautiful rocks and pebbles polished by the force of the water brushing the rocks against each other.

Before the river's powerful current transformed these rocks into beautiful treasures to be discovered by my eight-year-old, the intense water pressure had to pound on the rubble for hundreds of years. It wasn't a gentle or pleasant process. And the inherent nature of the stones didn't change; they were still the same old rocks. And yet, through an intense and even fierce process, what once was average and easy to overlook had become a young girl's prize.

Because the process is so unbearably slow, we often miss the incredible changes that life's erosion is causing in us. If we can patiently endure and trust that God has our back through our trials, we will start to discover hidden strengths and qualities that we didn't know we had before.

We can rejoice, too, when we run into problems and trials, for we know that they help us develop endurance. And endurance develops strength of character, and character strengthens our confident hope of salvation. (Romans 5:3-4)

We give great honor to those who endure under suffering. For instance, you know about Job, a man of great endurance. You can see how the Lord was kind to him at the end, for the Lord is full of tenderness and mercy. (James 5:11)

CHAPTER 7:
ACTIVE VS. PASSIVE PATIENCE

Patience is the quality which makes a man able, not simply to suffer things but to vanquish them. William Barclay

If you're running a 26-mile marathon, remember that every mile is run one step at a time. If you are writing a book, do it one page at a time. If you're trying to master a new language, try it one word at a time. There are 365 days in the average year. Divide any project by 365 and you'll find that no job is all that intimidating. Charles Swindoll

Although the word 'patience' suggests a state where you are sitting around waiting for something to happen, God's version of it demands a more active role. For example, if you lose your job, should you sit patiently at home in front of the TV waiting for the perfect job to fall in your lap? Or do you need to seek out new opportunities? If you are sick, do you shut off all access to doctors or other medical assistance, or do you try whatever it takes to get better?

Passive patience does little more than consume time. A good comparison may be a prisoner of war, waiting to be rescued.

We are often captivated into believing that there is little that we can or should do than to wait around for things to change.

Even a prisoner of war can do something. I love the story that James Ray tells about the six years he was a POW during the Vietnam War. During this time, the prisoners whispered Bible verses back and forth, an act that became vital to their daily existence. There wasn't much they could do, but the prisoners did what they could, and the shared verses became constant assurances of God's love and care.

Active patience, then, is to wait without complaint, but always aiming for the victory. That's why you find it described in the Bible as a race - where you never become hopeless, or even just try to hold your own. No, the goal with active patience is to make actual progress toward the objective every day.

...let us strip off every weight that slows us down, especially the sin that so easily trips us up. And let us run with endurance the race God has set before us. We do this by keeping our eyes on Jesus, the champion who initiates and perfects our faith. (Hebrews 12:1-2)

No, dear brothers and sisters, I have not achieved it, but I focus on this one thing: Forgetting the past and looking forward to what lies ahead, I press on to reach the end of the race and receive the heavenly prize for which God, through Christ Jesus, is calling us. (Philippians 3:13-14)

Remember Joseph who we met earlier? Well, he learned a lot of his patience from his father, Jacob, who had his share of trials to endure. Jacob was the twin brother of Isaac, the son of Abraham. Jacob did a foolish thing and got his brother, Esau, mad at him, and so Jacob chose to escape his homeland to let things cool off. All that is a tale that could consume a whole different book, but our story begins by a well in the land of Haran.

Jacob had escaped home and headed toward mom and dad's

ancestral home. While resting by the well, Jacob fell head over heels in love with his cousin, Rachel (which was perfectly acceptable back in Jacob's day). He spent a month with Rachel and her relatives, before asking Rachel's dad, Laban, if they could get married.

I know what you are thinking. Waiting a month to get married doesn't sound very patient to me, either. When it comes to MY daughter, I plan on making the guy wait at least a couple decades to make sure he is the right one for her! And maybe Laban had that in mind when he told Jacob he could marry Rachel in seven years.

The truth is, Laban was one crafty dude, and he had discovered that Jacob was an excellent shepherd. The herds thrived under his care, and Laban tied up his obedience for seven years by making Jacob work for Rachel.

For Jacob, a man smitten, the seven years flew by, and it was soon time to marry the woman he loved. But alas, Laban pulled a fast one on Jacob and switched sisters at the wedding. The result: Jacob ended up marrying Leah, Rachel's older sister instead.

Honestly, modern me can't figure out how this happened. I have seen some full wedding dresses in my day, but even if they hid Leah's identity during the marriage, how were they able to pull it off on the wedding night? Jacob must have been drunk that day is all I can say!

At any rate, the ruse worked, and Jacob woke up married to Leah, not Rachel. Jacob's only alternative, according to Laban, was to stay and work for him another seven years to pay for Rachel as well. Oh, don't worry, Laban did have a heart. Jacob and Rachel married right away, and Jacob paid off his debt in arrears. Laban was surely one crafty fellow!

So Jacob worked obediently with Laban's herds over the next seven years, and they grew and flourished. As did Jacob's family. Leah, a baby making machine, entered into a not-so-silent war with Rachel over who could produce the best offspring. When the competition got ferocious, they had Jacob sleep with their maids too. Frankly, I have no clue how Jacob had any time to work with the herds of sheep. He was too busy producing 13 kids over the next seven years (one of which was Joseph of the many dreams).

When Jacob's seven years servitude was up, he was ready to leave. While Jacob had worked for the past fourteen years, he had little to show for it but two wives, two "maids" and thirteen hungry kids, twelve of them boys. He had to make some money!

So what happens? Crafty Laban hires him to work the fields and offers a portion of the flock as pay. Any part of the herd that was spotted or marked could be Jacob's. Jacob agreed and immediately started studying up on cross-breeding techniques. Soon, Jacob's flocks were growing at a rapid rate. Laban, unhappy with the thought of losing his prize shepherd, changed the terms of his wages ten times over the next six years.

Meanwhile, Jacob worked without complaint through terrible weather, tolerated the theft of his flocks by Laban's staff, and lost sleep while guarding against further theft and loss. He managed the feud between his wives and was a father to all those kids. Still Jacob patiently persevered until the time he and his family were finally able to return to his home.

How was he able to be so patient? Flash back twenty years to a few weeks before Jacob met Rachel at the well. He was traveling toward Haran and stopped to rest for the night. Jacob lay his head on a stone scattered by the road, and fell asleep:

From "The Message, Genesis 28:12-22:

And he dreamed: A stairway was set on the ground, and it reached all the way to the sky; angels of God were going up and going down on it.

Then God was right before him, saying, "I am God, the God of Abraham your father and the God of Isaac. I'm giving the ground on which you are sleeping to you and to your descendants. Your descendants will be as the dust of the Earth; they'll stretch from west to east and from north to south. All the families of the Earth will bless themselves in you and your descendants. Yes. I'll stay with you; I'll protect you wherever you go, and I'll bring you back to this very ground. I'll stick with you until I've done everything I promised you."

Jacob woke up from his sleep. He said, "God is in this place—truly. And I didn't even know it!" He was terrified. He whispered in awe, "Incredible. Wonderful. Holy. This is God's House. This is the Gate of Heaven."

Jacob was up first thing in the morning. He took the stone he had used for his pillow and stood it up as a memorial pillar and poured oil over it. He christened the place Bethel (God's House). The name of the town had been Luz until then.

Jacob vowed a vow: "If God stands by me and protects me on this journey in which I'm setting out, keeps me in food and clothing, and brings me back in one piece to my father's house, this God will be my God. This stone that I have set up as a memorial pillar will mark this as a place where God lives. And everything you give me, I'll return a tenth to you."

Jacob could wait patiently for the time he and his family would return home by staying focused on God's promise to protect Jacob and stick with him through thick and through thin. A great reminder for all of us.

But another important lesson Jacob gives us is that while indentured to Laban, he didn't just sit back and wait for it to be over. He proactively learned the entire business of sheep herding. Not only did he learn how to manage a herd, but how to handle it in such a way that it flourished and grew.

Jacob learned how to communicate effectively with people, including a father-in-law whose sole aim was to detain him in Haran as long as possible. And he learned the complicated profession of cross-breeding to build his personal flocks in spite of his father-in-law's deceit. In other words, Jacob was patient but continued to strive toward his end goal of returning home.

It is this type of active patience that will see us through each day that we have to wait. It is an optimistic approach to the day that keeps us moving forward in pursuit of our goals.

CHAPTER 8:
STAYING OPTIMISTIC WHILE ENDURING TRIALS OF CIRCUMSTANCE

Active patience requires many other positive traits, including determination, endurance, compassion (Jacob must have been able to feel compassion for Laban all those years despite his poor treatment), and, most of all, faith. Each of these traits come from the root of positive, optimistic thinking. If we can improve our ability to think positively, we will come a long way in our quest to become more actively patient with our circumstances.

The pessimist sees the difficulty in every opportunity. The optimist sees the opportunity in every difficulty. Winston Churchill

When dealing with situations that seem out of our control, we will all have the occasional negative thoughts. Consider the story of Job for a moment. Job is possibly the most well-known example of patience under extreme trials in the Bible, with an entire book dedicated to his story. An interesting lesson from Job is that, while he remained committed to God throughout his trials, that didn't stop him from crying out in despair. He was as human as we are, and just because we are Christians doesn't mean we won't be scared, anxious and disappointed. God is okay with us calling out to him in our pain.

Nevertheless, always dwelling on the negative side of the equation will not help us develop patience. It just gives Satan a more fertile field to plant his seeds. Our thoughts are what drive our emotions, and negative and irrational thinking will lead to unhealthy emotional states. Here are some ways to help shape your thought patterns to be more positive and less negative.

<u>Declare emotional independence from the situation</u>. Eleanor Roosevelt once said, *"No one can make you feel inferior without your consent."* The truth is that regardless of what happens to you, your emotions are not determined by the circumstance or what others think, say, or do. You have the choice about how you will feel at any given time.

Don't take things people say and negative things that happen in your life personally. But make sure to take all the wonderful compliments you receive and positive events that occur in your life very personally! You have the control to accept what you hear and experience or not to. By allowing the positive and rejecting the negative, you will attract more of the former and less of the latter into your life.

<u>Spend each day as if it were the day before vacation</u>. Think back to the last vacation you took. The day before, weren't you excited and optimistic over what was in store? When we prepare for a holiday, we look forward to the adventure ahead; we don't fear what will happen. That is the perfect attitude to bring with us every day, whatever the day may bring.

Rid yourself of catastrophic talk. As discussed in Chapter 4, the words we use to describe an experience can make all the difference in the world. It won't make it better to zero in on how bad a situation is, or use highly negative words to describe it. It just deteriorates your already weak emotional state and your capacity to handle the situation, causing even more negative results. So instead of thinking and speaking in black or white: "this is a DISASTER!", try to see it in shades of gray: "this sure is a setback, what a challenge."

Beware of the "Yabbut!" "Yabbut" has killed many a great idea and instantly adds a negative vibration to a situation. I'm sure it's happened to you before: you have an excellent idea; you spell it out with great enthusiasm, and get in return: "Yabbut, we can't do that because..." Try to say "yes, and..." instead of "Yabutt." It keeps a positive charge in the air and opens the possibilities of new solutions.

Similarly, work toward describing your present how you want your future to become. If someone says "Hi, How are you?" give up the standard "fine" and answer "Terrific, never better!" Soon you will find that you are, indeed, feeling fabulous!

Finally, it's a good idea to rid your talk of all "lemon words." Those of us with children know that a "lemon word" is a profane statement. You know...one that makes your mouth pucker up when it is said! But we aren't just talking four-letter words here. Even socially acceptable words and phrases such as "shut up," "stupid," and "hate" have no place in an optimistic person's vocabulary. Be creative instead and find more positively charged and empowering words to describe what you are thinking.

Don't give in to Hopelessness. "I can't take this anymore," or "I don't think I can go another day," don't help improve your situation at all. The mere fact that you are standing there making such a statement proves you wrong. You have certainly been able to take everything that has been dished out so far! And the truth is: *If God is for you, who can be against you? (Romans 8:31)*

Hopelessness creates the most negative vibrational pull there is, and to succumb to it will eventually drag you under to a place from which you can't recover. Focus on God's promises and prepare some positive declarations to help pull you out from the hopeless cycle; this will help you to build the optimistic patience you need to overcome your circumstances.

You are the God who saves me. All day long I put my hope in you. (Psalm 25:5)

Let all that I am wait quietly before God, for my hope is in him. (Psalm 62:5)

For I can do everything through Christ, who gives me strength! (Philippians 4:13)

But those who trust in the Lord will find new strength. They will soar high on wings like eagles. They will run and not grow weary. They will walk and not faint. (Isaiah 40:31)

He will wipe every tear from their eyes, and there will be no more death or sorrow or crying or pain. All these things are gone forever. (Revelation 21:4)

For nothing is impossible with God! (Luke 1:37)

For God loved the world so much that he gave his one and only Son, so that everyone who believes in him will not perish but have eternal life. (John 3:16)

CHAPTER 9:
OVERCOMING OTHER CHALLENGES WITH OUR CIRCUMSTANCES

As optimistic as we may be, we are sure to encounter challenges that will try our ability to practice active patience during troublesome situations.

The first challenge to overcome is to accept that, despite the goals we may have set or the outcome we hope to attain from a situation, we have no guarantee that God will satisfy our desires. We might not get that dream job or be cured of our illness. While God can and has performed miracles, He isn't a genie up in the sky booming "YOUR WISH IS MY COMMAND!" to everything we may want.

God is sovereign and because of that knows best of all how to achieve His plans. And the truth is that most of the circumstances that require our patience aren't regarding specific promises from God. God has promised to meet our needs, but that isn't a guarantee that all of our wishes will come true.

Take delight in the Lord, and he will give you your heart's desires. (Psalm 37:4)

It's easy to interpret the above verse to mean we can get whatever we want if we just believe enough, but that thinking has a few flaws. First, it doesn't take into consideration the first part of the verse, that we should take delight in the Lord. In other words, trust that His plan is primary, not our desires.

Second, we may not even know what the desires of our heart are. We are bombarded daily with worldly influences and the devil's prodding. While we may believe that one thing is what we want in life, we might be missing out on something even better. Is the first the desire of our heart just because it is known? Who better, God or us, to know what will make us truly happy?

I think about a friend of mine who was feeling discouraged in life. His work wasn't satisfying, and that frustration was starting to spill over into his family and personal life as well. He began to self-medicate with too much TV and rich food. Over time, he became more and more out of shape and started to put on the pounds. That added stress did little to improve his attitude toward life.

Then, one day he was hit with a case of gout. You may be aware that gout is an inflammatory condition that affects the foot. It is very painful and can spread all the way up the leg, causing extreme discomfort, to the point where concentration on anything else is nearly impossible.

My friend saw his doctor, who frankly told him it was the wrong food and lifestyle choices that were giving him his pain, and challenged him to clean up his eating habits and get healthy again. The alternative: a future of painful gout attacks.

He agreed to give it a try, but like breaking free of any

stronghold, it wasn't easy. He went through the entire grief process. Denial: "It isn't what I eat, maybe I have a broken ankle or a tumor..." Anger: "Why did this happen to me?" Bargaining: "Okay, I'll be good for a month, then I can go back to my old ways..." Depression: "I'm never going to be able to eat anything but salad for the rest of my life." And finally, Acceptance: "Whole grain is not so bad, and it fills me up for a long time!"

In just three short weeks, my friend is reporting not only much less pain from gout but also a fresh and more creative outlook on his work and with his family and friends. His life is back on the right track, and some of his stalled dreams have revived.

My point with this story isn't to start eating more healthy (although this is not a bad idea), but to ask you to understand that sin and Satan's attempts to derail us keep us chained to the mundane when God has greater things in store for us. So even if we don't get the desires of our heart, we shouldn't lose patience or get angry with God. He knows what the real desires of our heart are, and will settle for nothing less. We shouldn't either.

CHAPTER 10:
DISCERNING GOD'S WILL

It's clear that in nearly every instance, active patience is preferable to passive patience. However, it is often hard to determine whether or not we are using active patience as we wait on God's timing, or trying to control a situation through our actions. The line is thin and easily blurred, even for the most diligent.

Discerning God's will can be one of the most elusive and frustrating parts of active patience. Suppose you are waiting to find your ideal mate. You meet several men you like. How do you know which (if any) is the one God has chosen for you? It can be so hard!

There aren't a lot of concrete techniques or strategies out there for effectively discerning the will of God. Each person communicates with God differently. And admitting that you talk to God regularly (and that you are listening for him to talk back) can be misinterpreted as a little crazy. So radio silence results.

But there are things you can put into practical use that will better open up the communication channels between you and God and help you to discern His will. Here are a few ideas.

<u>Make Jesus Your All Time Mentor</u>. "What Would Jesus Do? " the title of a book by Charles Sheldon, as well as the phrase stamped on countless bracelets, t-shirts, and Christian schwag is the right question to ask. When we have a mentor we trust, it is common to think about how they would react in a situation before we respond. Jesus tells us in John 14:6-7 that He is our all-time mentor in life: "I am the way, the truth, and the life. No one can come to the Father except through me. If you had known me, you would know who my Father is. From now on, you do know him and have seen him!"

But we live in the modern world, and He came from a simpler time! How can we know what Jesus would have done in our situation?

While it is true that the period Jesus lived in was less technologically advanced, people were still people, and there was plenty of modern day intrigue that occurred. They still struggled with hatred, jealousy, greed, lust, and dishonesty the same as today. And while Jesus' teachings to his disciples and other followers may not explicitly tie to something we are struggling with today, there are plenty of general guidelines in the Bible that we can apply to our personal circumstances.

In Psalm 119:105, David tells the Lord: *"Your word is a lamp to my feet and a light for my path."* Reading and studying the Bible will strengthen our relationship with Jesus, which will help us discern His will. Just as working with and spending time with a mentor helps us to learn how to succeed in a particular profession, spending time in God's word will help us to find out how to succeed at life.

<u>Seek the Advice and Counsel of Others</u>. God has placed

advisors and other godly people in our lives to help us to discern His will for us. Maybe it is someone close to you such as your spouse, pastor or another good friend. But you can also get advice and counsel by reading or listening to Christian authors and speakers. Frequently, I find that when I am struggling with a problem or concern, I may be talking to, reading or listening to a mentor on an entirely different subject when the solution to the problem reveals itself. God can work through our mentor's words to help us to understand our problems better, even if we don't share the specifics. Be open to these moments by always filling and refilling your heart and mind with more God-inspired information.

Pray, whenever you need God's guidance and direction: "If you need wisdom, ask our generous God, and he will give it to you. He will not rebuke you for asking." (James 1:5). We never have to worry about asking a dumb question or feeling unworthy to ask God for what we need and want. God wants us to pray about everything - as that is our primary form of communication with Him!

Listen For God to Speak Through Your Circumstances.
If we believe that God is perfect and that He has a plan for us, then we have to believe that God is in control of our lives - regardless of our circumstances. We may be in an uncomfortable place - we have lost our job or had a fight with a good friend. Even when we are sick with little chance of recovery or going through a financial crisis, God is in control of our lives.

I don't believe that God is the one that causes those bad things to happen to us. We've lived in a sinful world since the fall of Adam and Eve and Satan is just loving the havoc he can create in our lives. But I don't think God sees what is happening with surprise or confusion about how something like that could happen. He didn't mess up, and He knows how what happened will work for the good of His ultimate plans. We can't see it, but we can believe in Him.

Additionally, God talks to us through the opportunities that come our way. It's unnecessary for us to stew and agonize over a potential opportunity. Remember the saying from the Sound of Music: "When a door closes, somewhere God opens a window." We should be on the lookout for those open windows and be willing to climb through them.

<u>Follow Your Conscience</u>. God has put into each one of us a "thermometer" that tells us whether a situation is right or wrong. Often overlooked, it is that feeling in your gut that tells you to do something or not to. When a contemplated action is wrong, you will feel uncomfortable, guilty or confused. When it is right, you feel excited, motivated, and at peace, all at the same time.

Be careful, though to always read your conscience in conjunction with the other tools God provides us for discerning His will. Satan can work in you to train your conscience for evil rather than good. Never stop praying and studying God's word together with following your conscience to know best what God wants you to do.

Above all, seek God's will with an open mind and a willingness to do anything for God, not just what we want or like to do. The goal isn't to get God to do what we want, but to get us to do what God wants. Remember, God loves you more than anything, and so if what you want is in line with what he wants, he won't deny you. *"You fathers—if your children ask for a fish, do you give them a snake instead? Or if they ask for an egg, do you give them a scorpion? Of course not! So if you sinful people know how to give good gifts to your children, how much more will your heavenly Father give the Holy Spirit to those who ask him." (Luke 11:11-13)*

CHAPTER 11:
PATIENCE WITH YOURSELF

"Have patience with all things, but chiefly have patience with yourself. Do not lose courage in considering your own imperfections but instantly set about remedying them – every day begin the task anew." Francis de Sales

Ultimately, any impatience - with others or with your circumstances, can be even further exacerbated if you are impatient with yourself. It's easy to blame another person or your circumstances rather than admit that you are disappointed with your performance. It's hard to live up to the standards you impose on yourself when you're not patient with yourself when you make mistakes. You waste valuable time beating yourself up.

Impatience with yourself can lead to frustration, anxiety, disappointment, lowered self-esteem, and all kinds of negative thoughts and feelings. You may even experience physical effects on your body, such as tensing in your neck and shoulders, extreme fatigue and incomplete breathing.

We'd all like to be perfect, but only God is perfect. We'd all like to avoid the discomfort of messing up, but that can't happen, either. The truth is, we are all just a work-in-progress.

For God is working in you, giving you the desire and the power to do what pleases him. (Philippians 2:13)

It is okay to acknowledge our weaknesses so that we can work to correct them. But impatience stems from dwelling on those weaknesses rather than saying "I may not be there yet, but I'm working on it." Don't let your mistakes and challenges cause you to lose your enthusiasm for personal improvement and spiritual growth.

God has high expectations for us, but he also knows we are going to mess up. God is the God of second chances, and He will always be patient with us. We need to follow his example and learn to be patient with ourselves.

Remember that God is the one doing the work in us. Keeping that in mind will help to lighten the burden we feel to get better faster. God will work in us on his own time, and all we can do is cooperate. We do that by building and improving on our talents and abilities so that we can become the best we can be.

And I am certain that God, who began the good work within you, will continue his work until it is finally finished on the day when Christ Jesus returns. (Philippians 1:6)

Is there anything that can help you become more patient with yourself? All of the strategies and techniques presented thus far can help in this area as well. Also, we all need to do our best to slowwww dowwwwwn. In our quest to get as much done in a day as humanly possible plus ten more things, it is very easy to get impatient with ourselves, especially if we can't focus on the things that matter to us. We get so busy doing what we have to do that there is little time for the things we want to do. And that makes us frustrated, unfulfilled, and yes, impatient with ourselves. Here are some ways to help us to slow down and focus on the things that matter to us:

<u>Release stress and anxiety</u>. Periodically throughout the day, take a quick assessment of your stress level. Do you have tense shoulders, arms, or legs? A headache? Having trouble concentrating on one thing? These are all signs of pent-up stress. I find when I am most stressed my breathing becomes very shallow, making it difficult to get enough air, and making me feel exhausted.

When we have built up stress and anxiety, impatience is a frequent result. It starts with ourselves, and our inability to "get it all done." Then it travels outwards to impatience toward other people and our circumstances.

It's important to remember to release the mounting stress throughout the day rather than wait for the volcanic explosion that will come if it builds up. Try to get some exercise each day and a healthy dose of motivation through God's word and other inspiring speakers and authors. If you feel stress starting to escalate, take several large, cleansing breaths and purposely slow your motions until you feel yourself calming.

Another thing that can help if you feel stress rising is to stop multi-tasking for a while. We are fortunate to live in an age where we can achieve multiple things at the same time through instant messaging, email, and other convenient technology. But long hours of piling one thing on top of another will take its toll. If you start to feel the stress of overload, pick just one task to work on for a half hour or until you feel yourself relaxing again.

Multi-task overload can even take over in the car; this is one of my weak spots. I drive many hours a day. On particularly busy days I have caught myself listening to the radio, trying to carry on a conversation, monitoring my text messages, taking notes on stray thoughts and reading my Kindle at stoplights; not to mention trying to be a good driver. I can almost see the stress expanding inside the car as I stack more and more on. It's a wonder that when I finally open the doors, the vehicle doesn't just combust. I am slowly learning to shut it all down and just 'drive' instead of trying to conduct an entire day's business in the car, which is helping to make me a more patient person all through the day.

<u>Build your confidence in yourself and your abilities</u>. Impatience with ourselves may happen when we feel that we don't have control of a situation and that we have been let down (or have let someone else down). We may even feel that our hands are tied. You want something to happen now, but you cannot seem to do anything to speed things up.

When this type of thinking overtakes you, it's time to sit back and remember something. Remember, you aren't in control, God is. You can't do anything on your own to speed things up or make it right, but you can do ALL things through Christ who gives you strength (Philippians 4: 13). God is on your side. God has chosen you, has created you, and you are a new creation in Him.

Blanket yourself in the knowledge that with God, all things will work out perfectly. Then go about your day with confidence and assurance in your God-given abilities. Don't fight or rail against it. Realize that patience and faith go hand in hand, and God is with you every step of the way. *For the Lord will be your confidence and will keep your foot from being caught. (Proverbs 3:26)*

<u>Develop Perseverance</u>. Active patience is critical when we are trying to be patient with ourselves. Nothing happens as quickly as we would like it to, and we must press on through the urge to quit. I keep a magnet on my refrigerator that says P.U.S.H.: Pray Until Something Happens. I often think of that

when I am discouraged with how long something is taking. C.S. Lewis said *"What saves a man is to take a step. Then another step."* And another, and another.

After all, consider the alternative. What will happen if you do quit?

Paul is a great example to us of the attitude of perseverance. Throughout his ministry, he was persecuted, thrown in jail many times, and disdained by many. He starved, he was cold, and he regularly traveled, enduring many hardships. He died a painful death when he was beheaded in Rome, not knowing if he ever actually reached his earthly goal. But Paul's attitude of perseverance lives on and is an example we can all follow. *No, dear brothers and sisters, I have not achieved it, but I focus on this one thing: Forgetting the past and looking forward to what lies ahead, I press on to reach the end of the race and receive the heavenly prize for which God, through Christ Jesus, is calling us. (Philippians 3:13-14)*

CHAPTER 12: STANDING FIRM

Have you ever been having a beautiful day, only to have one thing happen that snaps your patience in an instant? Whoever, or whatever in your way becomes an unsuspecting target for your irritation and anger. That's the ultimate fight of good vs. evil between the author of patience; God, and the custodian of impatience; the Devil. Satan will use any tool he can find to separate us from God, and he has discovered that messing with our patience is an excellent way to distract us away from God's protection.

Not to get caught up in the macabre, but we do need to be aware that unseen forces are fighting for our allegiance. Make no mistake, when we demonstrate impatience we are the victim of spiritual warfare. And Satan is persistent in his war against God.

The closer your relationship with God becomes, the harder Satan will work to win you over to his side. When we are new in our relationships with God, the temptations to stray are big and easy to identify. But as we become more mature, the Devil starts working smarter, adding even more little annoyances and frustrations into our lives that test our patience and tempt us away from the way God wants us to live.

The sad truth is that life will be hard. Being a Christian will be hard. Things won't always go as we planned or when we planned. *Yes, and everyone who wants to live a godly life in Christ Jesus will suffer persecution. (2 Timothy 3:12)* But there is good news, and we are not at the mercy of Satan's war against God. Just as Job chose God despite all the Devil's temptations to stray, the choice is ultimately ours. We decide to be patient in our walk with God and to demonstrate that patience toward other people, our circumstances, and even towards ourselves.

I'm sure that Paul didn't want to suffer persecution and prison as much as he did. I'm sure he missed his cushy life before he accepted Christ and at times felt like his mission to spread the news of Jesus Christ was just too hard and took too long. But once Paul chose his goals, it was possible to look past the immediate trouble and persevere toward achieving those goals. In Romans 8:35-37 he shares with us his secret: that no one can separate us from our God and His plans for us. Only we can do that:

Can anything ever separate us from Christ's love? Does it mean he no longer loves us if we have trouble or calamity, or are persecuted, or hungry, or destitute, or in danger, or threatened with death? (As the Scriptures say, "For your sake we are killed every day; we are being slaughtered like sheep."No, despite all these things, overwhelming victory is ours through Christ, who loved us.

If Satan works so hard to develop our impatience, it stands to reason that by strengthening our ability to be patient we are drawing closer to our relationship with God. The world works in Satan's time, but our goals should be to succeed in God's time. By staying aware and working towards active patience with others, our circumstances and ourselves, we will reach the victory God has planned for us.

By standing firm, you will win your souls. (Luke 21: 19)

So let it grow, for when your endurance is fully developed, you will be perfect and complete, needing nothing. (James 1: 4)

While this is the end of the book, I hope you will stay in touch! If you enjoyed *Developing Patience and Perseverance in an Impatient World*, please take the time to give me a review. Very few people take the time, so it is a really big deal if you do. I very much appreciate it. To leave a review, please visit my Author page on **amazon.com/author/susanleebooks**

Please connect with me at **ProduceMyBook.com/gloabonusreg**, or email me at **Crew@ProduceMyBook.com**

Be sure to visit **ProduceMyBook.com** to learn how you can FINALLY get the book inside you written and produced!

ProduceMyBook.com: Concept to customer non-fiction books in as little as 8 weeks without the author ever typing a word of the manuscript!

Recommended Reading:

God's Law of Attraction: The Believer's Guide to Success and Fulfillment, by Susan Lee, available on Amazon.com

Experience God's Law of Attraction Through Bible Verses and Spiritual Affirmations, by Susan Lee, available on Amazon.com

Devotionals Reflecting on God's Power: What the Bible Teaches Us About Praise, Forgiveness, and More, by Susan Lee, available on Amazon.com

FREE BONUS!

Don't Forget to download your free bonus!

God's Law of Attraction Worksheets which will help you determine your goals, create positive affirmations, and combat negative beliefs.

Treasury of God's Promises is a collection of Bible verses that will help you focus on God's positive message.
Quotable Quotes is a selection of affirming quotes that will help you to keep God's powerful word in your heart.

In addition, you will be registered to receive new bonuses and gifts as they are added. To get all three gifts, just visit **ProduceMyBook.com/gloabonusreg**

Made in the USA
San Bernardino, CA
05 December 2018